BEDTIME STORIES FOR KIDS AGED 3-12

BY

Dr. Stacy Holcolm

Table of Contents

Introduction

Introduction

Young children often enjoy bedtime stories, and it has become a traditional way to put their curious minds to rest. Besides making them go to bed with a smile, bedtime stories help their mental and social development in a very subtle yet powerful way. So, make sure to read your child a story to bed whenever you can!

Chapter 1
Story of Pinocchio

Once upon a time, there lived a man called Geppetto. He was old and lived without anyone else. He had no group of his own.

Geppetto was a craftsman. He wanted to make stuff from wood. At some point, he remembered to put a manikin together with wood. He said, "I will make a young man and will call him 'Pinocchio.'

To begin with, Geppetto made a few wooden legs and arms. From that point forward, he made the body, and he included hands and feet. At long last, he made a young man's head. Geppetto made Pinocchio's eyes, mouth, and nose. From that point forward, he made his ears. Geppetto managed out constantly on his wooden manikin. He told himself, "I wish Pinocchio were a genuine kid."

A pixie heard Geppetto's desire. She chose to give into his desire and make the wooden manikin show some major signs of life. She shared with Pinocchio, "You should vow to be a decent and legitimate kid."

The following day, Geppetto was exceptionally glad to hear Pinocchio talk. He cherished
 his wooden child without question. Geppetto grinned. "Presently you can go to class with a wide range of various young men!". At school, Pinocchio saw that the wide range of various kids had genuine arms and legs. They were not made of wood. He was unique.

Pinocchio could have done without school. He could have done without getting his work done. His educator inquired, "Where is your schoolwork, Pinocchio?" He lied, "A whale ate it." Each time he lied, his nose developed longer.

Pinocchio could have done without that he was not the same as the other young men. At some point, he was furious and pushed one more kid over. His educator asked,"Did you push him over, Pinocchio?" Pinocchio lied, "In the event that wasn't me." Each time he lied, his nose developed longer.

At some point, Pinocchio chose to stow away from his educator. He concealed inside a major toy box, yet he was unable to get back out. He yelled, "Someone help me!' The pixie showed up. "For what reason are you stowing away, Pinocchio?" Pinocchio began to lie. His wooden nose developed increasingly long. His nose developed up to a tree limb.

The pixie said, "For what reason are you lying?" Pinocchio cried, "Please accept my apologies! | vow to at absolutely no point ever lie in the future.' The pixie grinned. "You can see a lie as simple as you can see the nose all over."

The pixie chose to help Pinocchio one final time. She set him free.
Pinocchio came out of the toy box. His educator inquired, "For what reason were you concealing the toy box, Pinocchio?" Pinocchio told the truth,"I could do without being unique." The educator grinned and said, "We are not quite the same as one another. That makes the world a fascinating spot to live." Pinocchio concluded that it wasn't so awful being unique. He began to play with different kids.

Pinocchio returned home to Geppetto. Pinocchio enlightened Geppetto concerning his new companions at school. The pixie perceived how Pinocchio had changed. She chose to transform him into a genuine kid. Pinocchio and Geppetto lived joyfully ever later.

Chapter 2

The wizard of oz

Story of Dorothy, a Kansas young lady who was conveyed by a cyclone to the remote place that is known for Oz. Dorothy needs to return home. She goes to the Emerald City to request the Wizard from Oz to help her. En route she meets a tin woodman,

Drothy and her little canine Toto lived in a little town in Kansas. She adored Toto definitely, and they would play with one another constantly.

On one occasion there was a terrible tornado. " We should get to the cellar, Toto!" cried Dorothy. Yet, it was too late.The spinning blowing wind lifted the farmhouse out of sight and took Dorothy

and Toto to the remote place that is
known for Oz.

the Magnificent Wizard of Oz
The farmhouse arrived with a shock.
Dorothy and Toto moved out of the
house and glanced around. " Goodness,
my, Toto! The house fell on somebody! I
didn't intend to harm anybody."
A blissful gathering of minuscule
individuals hurried up to Dorothy. "
Welcome to Oz! We are the Munchkins,
and that individual you arrived on was
the Underhanded Witch of the East. You
have liberated us from her devilish spell
until the end of time! Much thanks to
you!"

Another witch showed up, yet this was
the Excellent Witch of the North.
"Dorothy, you were extremely daring to
free the Munchkins. Assuming there is
any blessing I can allow, simply inquire."
"Might you at any point show me the
way back to Kansas?" asked Dorothy.

"Just the Wizard of Oz can assist you
with that. Yet, here, take these
enchanted silver shoes that had a place
with the Shrewd Witch of the East. They
might be useful to you later on.
Presently follow Yellow Block Street the
entire way to the Emerald City. There
you will track down the Wizard of Oz.

Out and about, Dorothy met a talking
scarecrow. " My head is brimming with
straw,and individuals believe I'm a
blockhead," moaned the Scarecrow. "I'd
give all that to have a cerebrum."
"I'll risk everything and the kitchen sink
of Oz could give you one," said Dorothy.
'I'm en route to see him right this
second. How about you join Toto and
me on our excursion?"

Further down the Yellow Block Street,
the small gathering found a Tin
Woodman who was rusted firm. After
Dorothy oiled the corroded joints, the
Tin Woodman had the option to openly

move. "Ok, thank you, young lady. I feel better as new — despite the fact that I actually have no heart. At the point when the tinsmith made me, he neglected to give me one."

"It seems like you really want to see the Wizard of Oz, as well!" cried Dorothy. "Show up with us!"

As they went via a backwoods, a major Lion hopped at Toto and thundered! "Don't even think about gnawing Toto!" yelled Dorothy.
The Lion flickered a tear and afterward looked down as if in disgrace.
Dorothy was stunned." For what reason you're barely anything yet a major defeatist!"
"I know," sniffed the Lion. "I'd very much want to have some mental fortitude."
"The Wizard of Oz will give Scarecrow a mind and me a heart," said the Tin Woodman. "Perhaps he can help you,too!"

So the Lion joined Dorothy, Toto, Scarecrow, and the Tin Woodman. Before long the Yellow Block Street guided them to the Emerald City. The safety officer at the entryway let Dorothy know that a couple of individuals at any point saw the Incomparable Oz yet that she and her companions had been conned by a group of people.

The little gathering apprehensively went into the huge Royal chamber and moved toward the Wizard. He paid attention to their solicitations and afterward replied, " I have heard that you destroyed the Underhanded Witch of the East. On the off chance that you can free us of her sister, the Malevolent Witch of the West, then, at that point, I will concede every one of your desires. Presently go!"

Be that as it may, the evil witch was chosen to kill Dorothy and her companions. She sent a bunch of starving wolves to gobble them up. "This is my fight!"said Tin Woodman. He swung his hatchet savagely. The frightened wolves turned and ran.

A shrieking, dark haze of wild birds obscured the sky." Crows!" hollered the Scarecrow, "This is my forte!" He waved his arms enthusiastically. " Boo!Go away! Shoo!"
"You saved us, Scarecrow," moaned Dorothy. " Bless your heart."

The Witch was enraged! She sent her winged monkeys to get the little gathering. Chatting monkeys dipped down, got the explorers, and flew back to the Malicious Witch's palace.

Dorothy was brought before the Insidious Witch of the West.
" In this way, you and your companions planned to annihilate me, eh ? Indeed, I've reversed the situation for every one

of you! The Tin Woodman is battered
and wound on a heap of extremely
sharp shakes. The Scarecrow is
completely unstuffed. I've accumulated
your Fearful Lion to a weighty truck.
" And with respect to you, my dear, you
and your irritating canine will use
whatever might remain of your life
working here in my palace!"

" You are exceptionally shrewd!" cried
Dorothy, and with that she tossed a can
of water all around the Witch.
" Gracious, no!" cried the malicious lady.
" Water will make me psychotic and
break up! Gracious, I'm contracting —
softening liquefying… "
Inside minutes the Insidious Witch was
just a puddle on the floor.

The Witch's slaves were presently free.
To show their appreciation, they fixed up
the Tin Woodman, filled the Scarecrow
with new straw, and delivered the Lion.
Not long from now Dorothy and her

companions were returning to the
Emerald City.

The Wizard was excited to see them."
You have done what I expected, and
you will be compensated'" So the
Scarecrow accepted his mind, the Tin
Woodman his heart and the lion his
fortitude.

"How might I return to Kansas?" asks
Dorothy.
The Wizard grinned. " You've had the
power from the beginning. Your
enchanted silver shoes will take you
anyplace you order!
Dorothy tragically went to her
companions. "It will be awesome to get
back, yet I will miss you all definitely ,"
She kissed them all goodbye. Then with
the assistance of her enchanted shoes,
Dorothy and Toto made a trip back to
their home in Kansas.

Chapter 3

Alice in wonderland

Alice is loosening up under a tree with her feline. She's exhausted essentially in light of the fact that nothing energizing at any point happens to her. Out of nowhere, she sees the most odd thing! A talking hare with a watch! "I'm late, I'm late for a vital date! " he continues to rehash. He runs past Alice and afterward into an opening in the ground.

Alice hops inside the opening and gets to a minuscule entryway. Through the keyhole, she sees the bunny in a delightful nursery. Yet , she is too large to even consider fitting through the entryway, and she starts to cry.

As she cries, she decreases and becomes more modest, until she winds up in a waterway of tears.

Alice swims to the way to the delightful nursery, and she meets a mouse and a dodo bird likewise swimming towards the entryway. They at long last land in the great nursery. The mouse and the dodo bird bid farewell and vanish.

Alice recognizes the white hare and follows him inside his home. She hydrates from a glass and develops as tall as a tree.

The bunny provides Alice with a piece of cake which makes the young lady little by and by. The hare runs off for the delightful nursery once more, and Alice pursues him.

As she goes through the blooms and the trees and bushes, she sees a tremendous mushroom. Sitting on the highest point of the mushroom, she sees a fairly immense, blue caterpillar. The caterpillar takes a gander at Alice and inquires, "Who are you? ""Where are you going? " Alice tells the caterpillar her name and asks about the white bunny.

She keeps strolling down the way and out of nowhere sees a tremendous feline happily. Alice gets some information about the white bunny, and the grinning feline illuminates Alice about a casual get-together. "Everybody is at the Frantic Hatter's casual get-together! " he says.

Alice shows up at the party, and she meets the Frantic Hatter and the Walk Rabbit. The two of them wear huge caps. The hatter asks Alice for what reason she doesn't wear a cap. Alice chooses now is the right time to go since she has no cap.

Alice shows up back again at the exquisite nursery. Three cards are painting the roses red. "For what reason would you say you are painting the roses red? " questions Alice. "The sovereign can't stand white roses. We need to paint them red, or she will remove our heads!.

Alice hears boisterous trumpet sounds and sees the sovereign entering the nursery. The sovereign looks exceptionally furious and yells, "Off with her head! "

Alice is going to answer to the sovereign, yet she sees the white bunny running towards her. "Stand by! " yells Alice.

"Where are you going?" The hare runs towards a little opening in the ground, and Alice follows. She starts to endlessly fall.

Alice stirs under a tree, next to her feline. Alice shakes her head and says, "What an outright exhilarating experience! " "It was all a dream"!.

Chapter 4

Ali baba and the forty hoodlums

Ali Baba, an unfortunate woodcutter finds a cavern brimming with gold and silver, concealed there by cheats.
He lets his sibling know who goes to look yet is caught in the cavern by the criminals. The sibling tells the pioneer Ali Baba has been taking the gold from the cavern. The pioneer intends to kill Ali Baba and his siblings and Forty hoodlums go to Ali Baba's home where they are concealed in huge oil containers in Ali baba's lawn. Alibaba's little girl hears them talking in the containers and recovers her loved ones.

Sometime in the distant past, an extremely quiet time ago, in the nation of sun,sand and pyramids, they carried on with an exceptionally unfortunate man. Ali Baba, was his name, he was poor however was blissful.

He had a caring spouse and an exquisite and shrewd girl named Leia. They resided in a little yellow stone house in a humble community close to certain slopes.
There were many trees in these slopes and every single day Ali Baba went there to cut wood. He rode to the slopes on his jackass, cut the wood, set it on the jackass' back and rode back to the town to sell it at the market.

One day when he was cleaving wood, Ali Baba heard a few ponies.
They were moving toward the slope.
'Ponies!' he thought. 'Ponies and men. I need to stow away.'

Rapidly he climbed a tree and hid in the green leaves. Right away he saw the men and the ponies. They halted close to his tree. Every one of the men were conveying packs. They looked extreme and perilous and Ali Baba realized that they were criminals.

The top of the cheats went up and remained before a major round stone. He set up his hands and cried, 'Open Sesame'.

The stone opened gradually and Ali Baba could see a cavern. It was enormous and exceptionally dull. Rapidly the hoodlums put their sacks in the cavern. Then, at that point, the pioneer set up his hands once more and said boisterously, 'Close Sesame'. The stone moved gradually and step by step back. The men moved on their ponies and rode away.

Ali Baba tensely held up in the tree until he could never again hear the ponies.
He was as yet frightened however he descended and strolled over to the stone.He set up his hands and murmured, 'Open Sesame'.
The stone moved and Ali Baba strolled into the cavern. He was unable to trust his eyes!
The cavern was loaded with gold and silver.Everywhere he looked he saw gold, gold boxes, gold creatures, and packs of gold and silver.

Rapidly Ali Baba took a pack of gold coins and ran out of the cavern.
'Close Sesame!' he cried and the stone moved back leisurely.
He raced to his jackass, which was all the while concealing in the trees, set the gold on its back, and rode home as fast as possible.

'Look what I have found,' he cried to his better half. At the point when she

thoroughly searched and took care of,
her eyes developed round with large
amazement.

Gold coins!' she said. 'Many gold coins!
Ali Baba, where did you get them?'
Ali Baba educated her regarding the
cheats and the stone and the cavern
loaded with gold and silver.'Oh, we will
get rich,' she said. 'Leia,' she cried to
her little girl.
'Leia, come here. Come and see what
your dad has found.'

At the point when Leia saw the gold
coins, she said joyfully, 'I will proceed to
get the weighing scales from Auntie
Kasima. We want to know the amount
they gauge. Then we will know how rich
we are.'
She went rapidly and returned with the
scales.
Ali Baba's better half gauged the coins.

'Gracious, we are rich, incredibly, rich!
We will purchase a fresh out of the box
new house, and I will purchase new
outfits for us all. Leia, return the scales
to your auntie and give her this gold
coin.'
That night, Auntie Kasima showed the
coin to her significant other, Ali Baba's
sibling, Kasim.'Look,' she said. 'Look
what we got from your sibling.'

Kasim took a gander at the gold coin
and murmured, 'Good gracious, is my
sibling a cheat?'
That evening he didn't rest soundly.
Next early morning he went to converse
with his sibling.
'Ali Baba, where did you get this gold
coin?' he addressed. 'Might it be said
that you are a hoodlum?'
Ali Baba snickered. 'No sibling, I'm not a
cheat, but rather I've found a cavern
where criminals conceal their gold.'

He informed Kasim concerning the
cavern and the cheats and the gold. He
educated him concerning the stone.
'I will take you there tomorrow,' he said.

Kasim returned home yet the entire
morning he pondered the cavern and
the gold.
'I would rather not hold on until
tomorrow, I can hardly hold on until
tomorrow! 'he thought.
So in the early evening he rode rapidly
to the cavern without anyone else.
He remained before the stone and
said,'Open Sesame'.
Wherever he looked he saw gold.
'Gold! Such a lot of gold!' he cried.'Oh,
I'm rich,very rich.

Unexpectedly he heard the sound of
ponies outside the cavern. He attempted
to stow away, yet he was past the point
of no return. The hoodlums, forty of
them, came into the cavern.

At the point when they saw Kasim,they
took out their long blades.
'Who are you?'cried the pioneer. 'What
are you doing in our cavern? Get him,
men. He is attempting to take our gold.'

'If it's not too much trouble, kindly don't
kill me!' Kasim cried. He was extremely
frightened.
'I would have rather not taken your gold.
I was simply looking. My sibling, Ali
Baba, let me know it was here. He
tracked down the cavern and took some
gold. Kindly, kindly don't kill me'
The head of the hoodlums said, 'Let us
know where your sibling lives, and you
can return home.'
Be that as it may, when Kasim told him,
he giggled a dreadful snicker.
Tie him up, men. We will track down this
Ali Baba and our gold. Then, at that
point, we will kill him and his sibling.'

The pioneer advised the criminals to get
forty major oil holders.

'Men, I will place oil in one container and you will conceal it in different containers. I will take the containers to Ali Baba's home. Then, around midnight, when everybody is dozing, I will open the containers.
You will move out and kill Ali Baba and his family and we will get our gold back.'

Then, at that point, the pioneer put oil in one container and the 39 cheats moved into the other 39 containers.
The pioneer put the oil containers onto the ponies and strolled with them to Ali Baba's home. He thumped on the entryway.
'Goodbye, kind companion. Could you at any point help me, please? I have come from a long way away to sell my oil at the market. It's currently evening and the market is shut. If it's not too much trouble, can my ponies and my oil containers remain in your lawn until the morning?'

'Goodness, indeed, they can remain here,' said Ali Baba, for he was a thoughtful man and he was dependably eager to assist individuals.

'What's more, you can rest in my home,' he shared with the pioneer.
Little did Ali Baba have any idea what the hoodlums were arranging.
After supper, the top of the hoodlums went into the nursery to address his men. 'Keep in mind,' he murmured into the containers.
'In the evening, open your container, move out, go into the house, kill Ali Baba and his family, and see as our gold.'

Soon thereafter, Leia went to get some oil. It was exceptionally peaceful in the lawn.
Out of nowhere she heard murmurs from the containers. 'It's chilly here.' 'I really want to move.'
Leia tuned in and understood.

The cheats from the cavern are in these
containers. I will show them a thing or
two,' she thought.
In the house she made some extremely
hot oil. Then, at that point, she put a
little in each container.
'Goodness, oof,' cried the hoodlums.
Individually they leaped out of the
containers and took off as quickly as
possible. Their chief took off as well.

They were so frightened, they ran for
quite a while before they halted. They
didn't return to Ali Baba's home and they
never returned to the cave again.

A couple of days later, when Ali Baba
was sure that the thieves were not
coming back, he went to the cave and
found his brother Kasim, cold, but living.

They cried together and then they
laughed together. Then they took some
more gold and went home. The two

families and all their friends were now
very rich and lived happily ever after.

Chapter 5
Story of Mary Poppins

When Wed Poppins shows up at Banks house, their kids Jane and Michael's lives are flipped around supernaturally. Mary Poppins takes the youngsters on the most additional common undertakings to a ride on a merry go round inside a walkway picture, to a roof of London. At the point when they are with Mary Poppins, the most mystical things appear to occur!

Hi, there! I go by Bert. I'm somewhat of a man-about town, you could say. I do what suits me - sell kites, clean fireplaces, or lay out pictures on walkways. Today it suits me to be a one-man-band. How about you

accompany me? London is luxurious
this season!

Here we are at Cherry Tree Path, and
around there is Number Seventeen,
where the Banks family lives. Quite
recently, something extremely surprising
- and very amazingthing occurred at the
Banks home.

Allow me to recount to you the story. Mr.
Banks worked the entire day in a bank,
and Mrs. Banks was generally occupied
with club gatherings and such, so Jane
and Michael, the Banks youngsters,
needed to have a caretaker, which is an
individual who cares for youngsters.
Jane and Michael had a few caretakers,
and on this exceptional day, the most
recent one had recently left, telling Mr.
and Mrs. Banks that they'd need to find
another person to care for their little
beasts!

Jane and Michael weren't exactly wicked. The Babysitter just misconstrued. She thought the youngsters had taken off from her, when all they'd done was follow their kite.

Presently Mr.and Mrs. Banks needed to track down still another babysitter. The method for doing that was to put an ad in the paper, calling for somebody firm and functional.

Jane and Michael, obviously, had their own thoughts regarding the sort of individual who ought to be their caretaker, and to help their dad they composed a commercial for him: " Needed: A Babysitter. Should have a good personality, blush cheeks, and be prepared to mess around."

At the point when Mr. Banks saw the kids' notice, he called it " senseless nonsense." He destroyed it, tossed it in the chimney, and composed the ad himself. In any case, late that evening an odd breeze blew down the Banks smokestack and conveyed the pieces up into the night sky.

The following morning, when Jane and Michael got up, the line of babysitters they saw from their window extended clear around the block! They were all ready to be evaluated by Mr. Banks, and a firm and reasonable part they were. Not a blushing cheek among them.

Jane checked out at the babysitters with consternation. " I don't grasp Michael. They're not what we publicized for by any means."

However, all at once a breeze began blowing from the east. Down Cherry Tree Path the east wind blew, expanding more and more grounded. At long last it picked up that large number of firm and reasonable babysitters and blew them away.

Prior to Mr. Banks even realized they were there, every single one of them was no more!

Jane and Michael watched in bliss from the play room window. Then, at that point, riding toward them on the east wind, an individual holding a dark umbrella drew nearer. " Goodness look, Michael! It's her! Our caretaker! Blushing cheeks and everything!"

The blushing cheeked individual arrived on the front doorstep of Number Seventeen. She expeditiously walked in and said, " Mr.Banks, I'm the new caretaker." And before Mr. Banks even realized what had occurred, she slid up the rail to the nursery.

" I am Mary Poppins," she expressed, removing her jacket and cap. "Go along, kids. We'll start with a game called 'We should Clean Up the Nursery.' "

Jane could have done without that. " Would you say you are certain it's a game, Mary Poppins?"

" That relies upon your perspective. In each occupation that should be finished, there is a piece of tomfoolery. You track down the tomfoolery and snap! The work's a game."

Mary Poppins snapped her fingers, and sufficiently sure, " We should Clean Up the Nursery" turned into a supernatural game. Toys set themselves aside, beds made themselves, garments hung themselves up, and soon the play room was flawless as a pin.

The youngsters were excited. " Mary Poppins, you're astounding!" " obviously. What's more, presently you should get some rest. Tomorrow we'll have an excursion in the recreation area."

The following day it fit me to be a walkway craftsman, and I was portraying pictures in chalk when I gazed upward and saw Mary Poppins and the kids.

" You're fortunate youngsters without a doubt! At the point when you're with Mary Poppins, wizardry simply appears to occur. What about a touch of enchantment at this moment, Mary Poppins? Nobody's looking."

" Indeed, assuming we should, we should. Presently line up, and hop!"

Unexpectedly we wound up inside one of my walkway pictures, at a region fair. Each of the four of us took a ride on a merry go round, and afterward Mary Poppins rode her pony right off the slide merry go round, and our own followed. We joined a fox chase, and entered a horse race. Gracious, we made some carefree memories!

That night when Mary Poppins wrapped the kids up, Jane had a solicitation. " Gracious, Mary Poppins, we had the most astonishing day! Guarantee you won't ever leave us!"

" That is a pie-hull guarantee - handily made, effectively broken. I will remain until the breeze changes. Presently nod off. Tomorrow you are going on a trip with your dad, to the bank where he works."

Jane and Michael were stunned. " Truly? Father has never taken us anyplace."

For sure, he wasn't excessively content with Mary Poppins when he had caught wind of the kids' new experience.

" Truly, Mary Poppins! The kids' excursions ought to be functional, instructive."

Furthermore, Mary Poppins concurred. " I very much see your point, Mr.Banks. Tomorrow the youngsters will be next to you."

As early as possible the following morning, the kids set out to manage an account with their dad. Michael had carried a few coins with him to purchase nourishment, however Mr. Banks wouldn't know about that. " You should place your cash in the bank where it will procure revenue. Give it to me!"

Out of nowhere, the trip with their dad lost all its commitment to tomfoolery, and Jane and Michael let go of his hands. They ran off and got themselves lost.

It was great that they ran into me. That day it fit me to be a stack clear, and the youngsters were satisfied to see me. However, they were as yet vexed. " Goodness, Bert! Father attempted to take Michael's cash! He could do without us by any means!"

I shut down thinking like that. " Your dad loves you without question. It's him I feel frustrated about. There he is the entire day in that chilly, wanton bank, and nothing to stay with except for cash."

That made them reconsider. Jane and Michael chose to apologize. " Go along, then, at that point," I said. " It's my day to clean your smokestack. I'll bring you back home."

However, before I really might begin on their stack, Mary Poppins had an unexpected treat for us. In a shimmering she whisked every one of us up the stack and out onto the housetop!

We looked out over the roofs of London.
``What a wonderful view," said I. " And
who will see it from up here yet the
birds, the stars and the fireplace
clears?"

We moved and sang and hosted an
ordinary get-together. At the point when
you're with Mary Poppins, the most
supernatural things appear to occur!

Jane and Michael felt improved after
their party on the roof, and they went
directly to their dad. Michael offered him
his coins to place in the bank. Mr. Banks
grinned.

" Keep your cash, Michael. I was just
doing what I trusted best for you, yet
presently I see that cash isn't simply
significant. It's having some good times
that counts at your age, and from here
on out, I will invest significantly more
energy with you both." And Mr.Banks

gave the kids an embrace and headed out to make them a kite.

Then the entire Banks family went to the recreation area together, without precedent for very lengthy. They flew their kite and lived it up. The breeze had changed, and everyone needed to fly a kite. I was the one in particular who saw Mary Poppins cruising ceaselessly on the west wind. " Farewell, Mary Poppins," I waved. " Don't remain excessively lengthy."

Chapter 6

Gulliver Travels

Gulliver was an exceptionally smart young fellow, who wanted to have experiences. He had a decent life, yet Gulliver needed to see the world.

Gulliver delighted in learning new dialects and meeting new individuals. Thus, when Gulliver could, he abandoned his life and went on journey across the ocean. He needed to meet new individuals and to see and learn new things. This story is about Gulliver's most prominent experience ever.When Gulliver left Britain for the South Oceans, he had no clue about the undertakings to come.

Gulliver and his group hopped on their boat the Antelope. They felt invigorated and prepared for their long excursion. Yet, subsequent to going for quite a while in horrible climate, things began to turn out badly.

The breeze blew hard and the oceans were hazardous. Gulliver was quick to see the huge stone before the Impala.

'The group battled contrary to the natural flow, however unexpectedly the Impala hit the stone. With a horrendous accident, the boat broke in two. Gulliver swam for his life in the ocean, He was terrified. The water was extremely profound and he was unable to feel the base.

Gulliver endlessly swam. He searched for the group, however he was unable to see them. He was distant from everyone else.

At the point when he showed up ashore, Gulliver lay near the ocean and fell into the most profound rest.
Gulliver woke gradually. He felt awful. He didn't have any idea where he was. He recalled the team and he felt miserable. Where could they have been?

He attempted to move his hand. He proved unable. He attempted to move his head, yet he proved unable. He attempted to move his legs and feet, yet he was unable to move any of his body whatsoever. It was blistering and Gulliver could feel the sun all over his body.

Was this a terrible dream? Then, at that point, Gulliver felt something continue on his leg. What was it? A little creature?
The thing moved gradually up Gulliver's body and remained on his chest.

Gulliver woke up and shouted out 'Whaaaaat? It was a little individual!

This individual was just 15 centimeters high. He looked irate and somewhat apprehensive. In his grasp, the minuscule man had a bow and bolt. He pointed it at Gulliver.

Gulliver couldn't accept the obvious reality! Out of nowhere, he felt more things continuing on his body. They were on his arms and legs and chest. There were a ton of the small individuals on Gulliver and they all had bows and bolts.

Gulliver yelled as uproariously as possible! He was unable to move and these little individuals needed to hurt him!

Gulliver heard small cries. At the point when he yelled, a portion of the little individuals tumbled to the ground.

Gulliver attempted to free his arms and legs, yet he was unable to move. He peered down and saw a ton of little ropes which fixed him to the ground.

He pulled his arm up as hard as possible and it came free. Then he did likewise with his legs.

Gulliver sat up and every one of the small individuals shouted out. To them, Gulliver was Gigantic!

Then Gulliver felt a shower of small bolts all over his body.

The little individuals feared Gulliver. Their bolts hurt him, however he was not apprehensive. He was recently drained thus, so ravenous.

He needed to address the little individuals, however he didn't comprehend their language and they didn't figure it out his. So he took a gander at them and highlighted his mouth. A little man in fine garments came towards Gulliver.

It was the Sovereign of the little individuals.

The Sovereign grinned at Gulliver. He advised the little individuals to drop their bows and bolts. Then, at that point, he addressed some of them and pointed. 'Presently they will get food,' thought Gulliver. His stomach made a boisterous commotion and a portion of the little individuals tumbled to the ground. They were terrified! Gulliver chuckled and the Head snickered with him.

'I will like it here,' said Gulliver. Furthermore, the Sovereign, who didn't grasp a word, snickered once more

Before long, the little individuals purchased food. Everything was small! They brought little chickens, small fish,

minuscule plates of bread, salad and
vegetables and small cakes and
desserts. It was all little, however they
brought A Great deal!

Gulliver felt far improved after a decent
supper. After some time, the little
individuals began to deal with where
Gulliver could sleep.They all brought
their beds and covers and set them up
to make a major bed for their new
companion.

Gulliver took in their language. The
name of the island, individuals told him,
was Lilliput. Individuals were Lilliputians.
Gulliver delighted in conversing with the
Lilliputians and playing with them! He
was so huge to them!

He purged his pockets and showed the
Lilliputians his watch.

They couldn't really accept the
commotion it made! He showed them a

few coins, which were close to as large
as they were! What's more, he showed
them his glasses, which to the
Lilliputians were enormous!
The Lilliputians cherished Gulliver.
Artists came and moved on his hands.
Young men and young ladies messed
around in his hair. Horse riders got
around his hands on their ponies.

The Lilliputians presented to him all the
food they could find for himself and they
made him some awesome new
garments.

Gulliver was extremely blissful, however
he was the sort of man who experiences
and he was prepared for another
experience now.

Gulliver addressed the Head and the
Ruler concurred. Gulliver was free! He
could go where he enjoyed.

Gulliver was energized! He chose to
visit the city. It was anything but a long
stroll for Gulliver. He just must be
exceptionally mindful so as not to step
on the little individuals who he met on
the way!

In the city, Gulliver visited the
Sovereign's castle. It was delightful, yet
exceptionally minuscule, so Gulliver
couldn't go inside,Then Gulliver had a
thought! I know!' Gulliver thought, 'I'll
step over the wall into the Sovereign's
nursery. Then, at that point, I'll rest and
glance through the window. The
Sovereign's better half giggled when she
saw him and she put her hand through
the window. Gulliver took the little hand
and kissed it.

Gulliver delighted in gathering
individuals, so he addressed many
individuals in the city. He discovered
that Lilliput was at battle with individuals

of Blefuscu, a little island close to
Lilliput.

The Head and every one individual of
Lilliput held up at the port. They saw the
boats before they saw Gulliver, who was
upto his chest in water.

Then, at that point, they heard Gulliver
shout out in his most intense voice,
"May the Sovereign of Lilliput live
forever!"
The Lilliputians applauded their little
hands and yelled as noisily as possible.
The conflict was finished!

'Much obliged to you Gulliver!' they
cried, When they generally yelled
together, their voices were extremely
clear!

Yet, certain individuals in Lilliput were
not exceptionally content with Gulliver.

The Ruler gave Gulliver all that he needed. Flimnap, the Sovereign's companion, felt Desirous of Gulliver.

'Gulliver is excessively huge!' he shared with the Sovereign. 'He eats excessively! He Is excessively expensive!'
Certain individuals said that Flimnap needed to hurt Gulliver. Gulliver was apprehensive. 'The time has come to leave Lilliput,' thought Gulliver. 'I might want to return home now '.

Gulliver told the Ruler and the Sovereign how he felt. They got it. 'You are a man who loves experiences, Gulliver,' they said. 'Perhaps it's the ideal opportunity for another one at this point.'

Gulliver lay on the ground to address them. He kissed their minuscule hands.

'Be that as it may, how might I leave?'
he asked them. 'I'm too huge for ships!
Furthermore, I can't swim the whole way
to Britain!'

'You helped us,' said the Sovereign.
'Furthermore, presently we will help
you!'

The Head requested that every one of
the Lilliputians meet up. 'We will
fabricate the greatest boat ever!' he
cried.

The Lilliputians buckled down for days
and evenings. They cut down their
biggest trees and conveyed the wood to
the port. They started to construct a
colossal boat for their gigantic
companion.
Gulliver helped, as well. He conveyed
the heaviest bits of wood and set them
up to make the boat.

Flimnap would have rather not helped, however he was blissful about Gulliver's arrangement. 'There will be more nourishment for us now!' he said 'There will be a greater amount of everything for us!

Different Lilliputians disagreed. The Head disagreed. They adored Gulliver and they maintained that he should remain. Yet, they got it. Gulliver had new spots to visit, new individuals to meet and new experiences to appreciate.

The Sovereign gave Gulliver a few little coins and an image of Gulliver in Lilliput with his companions. 'Much thanks to you,' said Gulliver, 'for everything.'

Gulliver was miserable. He was additionally frightened. His boat was brilliant, yet it was still little for him. 'I will not return as far as possible once again to Britain in this,' he thought.

Gulliver strolled into the water. He
hauled the boat behind him. Then he
moved inside and started the journey
home.

Gulliver traversed the oceans for a long
time. He was eager, parched and tired.
And afterward something superb
happened Gulliver saw a little island
before him!
He maneuvered his boat onto the ocean
side and strolled onto the sand. His legs
felt frail. He tumbled to the ground and
dozed for quite a while.

At the point when Gulliver woke, the sun
was blistering all over.

In any case, Guiliver was separated
from everyone else and he felt
somewhat miserable without his small
companions.

Gulliver discovered some food on the island. He ate and felt improved. He sat on the sand and watched out to the ocean.

Out of nowhere, he saw a colossal boat in the water. It was exceptionally distant from him, however he could simply see … It was an English boat!

'Finally!' he cried. 'I'm returning home!'

At the point when the boat halted close to the island, Gulliver endlessly swam and yelled as uproariously as possible. 'Kindly don't leave me here!' he cried.

The boat's team heard him and they helped him onto the boat. Gulliver hydrated and ate a feast. Then he recounted to the group his story. 'It feels better to communicate in English!' he said.

The group were thoughtful and they listened well. Yet, they couldn't trust their ears!
'Minuscule individuals!' they said, '15 centimeters high? How could this be valid?'

'It is valid!' cried Gulliver. He began to feel irate. 'Is there any good reason why you won't trust me?'
Then Gulliver recollected. He put his hand in his pocket and took out the minuscule coins and the image of him in Lilliput with his little companions close to him. He showed them to the group.
The group's eyes were wide. 'Perhaps this story is valid!' they said.

At the point when Gulliver got back to England
His ears became bored of the English language. His eyes became bored of the people, who all looked the same to him. He wanted to see new things, hear new things and learn new things.

This was Gulliver. He loved adventures.

Chapter 7

Princess and the Magical Ring

One fine day, the princess of the kingdom of Norfolk found a ring while in the palace's garden. When she inquired about the ring with her father, he informed her that it would bring her five special powers:

The ability to get sound sleep.

The ability to make fire without a flint.

The ability to grow any crop of her choice.

The ability to make it rain even without clouds in the sky.

The ability to sing like an enchanted siren.

The fifth was the princess' most enjoyed power. She would keep singing for long, hoping that someday, a charming prince would fall for her beautiful voice.

One dark day, the kingdom got jinxed with a witch's spell. It affected everyone except the princess. The witch deprived the kingdom of everything it had, including fire, the sun, the rains, and the crops. The miserable state of her country saddened the princess. But, all she had to help her kingdom were her five special powers! A spontaneous idea popped into her mind – she rushed to the balcony and started singing. The princess sang for months, all day and night. She didn't stop even when her parents asked her. After about a year of singing, the kingdom normalised. But simultaneously, the princess disappeared in the winds. The kingdom was restored to its original glory because of the princess' sacrifices.

Chapter 8

The Lonely Princess

The Kingdom of Glora was home to Princess Isabella, a friendly young lady who was loved by the whole kingdom. She had two elder sisters, Rose and Juliette, but she was nothing like them. Rose was quite charming, but she was no match to Juliette. Nevertheless, they were both mean to Isabella because they were considered conventionally beautiful. They teased Isabella for her plain appearance and simplicity, and always made fun of her for playing with her toys. They coaxed her to dress up more, but Isabella paid no heed to her sisters and continued to play with her toys. She loved her dolls as they never called her names, but she often felt lonely. King Paul, her father, was distressed at the sorrow of his youngest child, and although he tried to spend his free time with her, he was often called

away for extended periods because of
his royal duties.

On a bright summer morning, the prince
of the Kingdom of Meadow-Hill,
Geoffrey, arrived in the Kingdom of
Glora, seeking a bride. He was a year
younger than Juliette, a year older than
Rose, and two years older than Isabella.
All the sisters were eager to meet the
handsome prince. Prince Geoffrey first
spoke to Juliette, praising her beautiful
tresses. Flattered, Juliette told him how
lovingly she took care of her hair.
Geoffrey soon got tired of the
conversation and tried to strike a
conversation with Rose. To impress the
young prince, Rose began describing
her father's court and talking about all
the famous personalities in it. When
Prince Geoffrey could hear no more, he
decided to meet Isabella. As soon as he
met her, he was awestruck by her
beauty. Juliette and Rose scoffed at
Isabelle, berating her unkempt hair.

When the prince said she had beautiful eyes, both Rose and Juliette declared that all the sisters had beautiful eyes. Prince Geoffrey said, "She is blessed with beautiful eyes indeed. But she plays with toys!" Juliette countered, trying to make young Isabella appear childish. "So what? Even I like playing with dolls." Taking out a small doll from his pocket, he introduced it to everyone as Jane, his oldest friend. Isabella, delighted, offered to introduce him to her friends. When he agreed, she led him into the garden, leaving behind her mean sisters.

Chapter 9

The Princess and the Pea

There once lived a prince who was in search of a suitable princess. He travelled across the seven seas in search of the right one, but he wasn't sure if the princesses he met were genuine. Disheartened, he eventually returned home.

One evening, there was a terrible thunderstorm. Having heard a knock on the door, the queen went to open it. A princess was standing there in soiled and muddy clothes. Her hair looked dirty; she was thoroughly drenched, and her shoes were covered in mud. She claimed to be a real princess. "We'll soon find out the truth," said the queen. The queen went to the bedroom and took all the mattresses off the bed. She then placed a pea at the bottom and laid twenty mattresses on top of it. Next, she placed twenty feathered beds on top of the mattresses. The princess was asked to sleep on the bed for the night. In the morning, the queen questioned the princess about the quality of her sleep. The princess replied, "I just couldn't sleep all night. God knows what, but there was something very hard on the bed." The queen then understood that she was indeed a real princess, as only a real princess would feel the discomfort through the twenty mattresses and feathered beds. Knowing that she was a real princess, the prince took her as his wife.

Chapter 10

The Princess and the Faithful Knight

Once upon a time, there was a princess whose beauty was the talk of not just her own, but many a land. As beautiful as she was, the princess had been raised to be fair and just. As the days went by, the happiness and the joy of her people became her only concern. One day, a prince arrived at the kingdom to court the princess. The two spent hours, days and weeks together. The princess had fallen in love with the charming prince.

One day, the prince took his princess to a shady grassland full of flowers located near the edge of the forest. He challenged the princess to pick out the rarest flower for him – the scarlet rose from the dense woods – if she truly loved him. The princess entered the woods to search for the scarlet rose. She loved the prince, and she would prove it to him. When she had almost given up, she saw a beautiful flower. The princess was fascinated by its beauty and reached out to touch it, but immediately fell asleep.

The prince suddenly appeared. He had planned to steal the riches and jewellery of the princess. He took the valuables and abandoned the princess. When the princess did not return to her father, the king sent his soldiers far and wide to look for her. After a long search, they discovered her in the meadow, covered in vine. His advisors discovered that she had touched a scarlet rose and thus couldn't be awakened. The king tried every possible measure and potion to wake her up, but nothing helped.

The disheartened king made it known that anyone who could wait by the princesses' side until she awoke would win her hand in marriage. Many suitors came drawn by the princesses' beauty, but she slept on, unaware. As time passed, her beauty faded, as did most suitors, except for one- a knight who had knelt at the princess' side and hadn't moved since the time he had arrived. When the princess woke up, she saw the strong knight kneeling by her side. He told her about the poison and the king's decree and declared his undying love for her. The king was overjoyed at having his daughter back, finding her a loving husband, and declared their wedding which took place the very next day.

Chapter 11

Princess Rose and the Golden Bird

Long ago in a faraway land there lived a beautiful princess who had lovely red hair, and loved roses. Her name was Princess Rose. Every evening, Princess Rose would come out on her balcony and clap her hands. On hearing her, a little golden bird would appear and sit on her shoulder. The princesses' hair would have a beautiful red glow, and she and the bird would sing a lullaby that would put everyone in the kingdom to sleep.

One day, a jealous witch cast a spell on princess Rose and turned her lovely red hair black. That night, when the bird and the princess sang, the people of the kingdom had nightmares and bad dreams. The bird told the princess to wash her hair in rose water, and all would be well again. The princess

washed her hair with rose water, and
people of the kingdom slept well.

When the evil witch heard this, she
turned princess Rose's hair black again;
and this time, she also made all the
roses in the land disappear. As princess
Rose wept in despair, a prince appeared
with a strand of red hair. When her tears
touched the hair, a beautiful red rose
bloomed, and princess Rose was able
to make her hair red again. The Prince
revealed that he and the princess had
exchanged a strand of hair as children
as a sign of loyalty..

The prince and princess Rose got
married and lived happily ever after, and
the evil witch was so furious at the
failure of her plan that she exploded into
a thousand pieces.

Tips to Remember When Reading a Bedtime Story to Your Child

Act like the Character

At the point when you get into the zone of the person, it makes your kid's creative mind take off. To make things really fascinating, you could ask your kid what he figures a person would seem like. Then, progress forward with that voice.

Make it intelligent

A ton of the narratives you read include scenes where characters conclude what they need to do. In such a case, you can ask your kid what he would do in the event that he was a person in the story. Like that, your kid will be associated with the story and you can likewise make sense of for him how certain activities have outcomes.

Everyday Daily practice
It assists them with fostering an
everyday practice that improves the
kid's bonding with the narrator.

Understanding readiness: it assists them
with teaching an interest in pursuing.

Perception and rationale: it further
develops their language abilities.

Correspondence: it makes the kid more
expressive and intelligent.

Ethics and values: it is an imaginative
means to guzzle virtues in youngsters.

CONCLUSION

Bedtime stories are more than just sharing a cute story. They are an important way to bond with your little one. There are many advantages of interacting with your child by way of reading bedtime stories.

I hope the aforementioned tips help you create a strong bond with your little ones.